LOVE THREADS

LOVE THREADS

Thomas Ramey Watson

Barn Swallow Media

LOVE THREADS

Barn Swallow Media
Denver, CO

Copyright © 2014 Thomas Ramey Watson
All rights reserved.
ISBN: 0-9818430-4-2
ISBN-13: 978-0-9818430-4-9
LCCN: 2014932156

LIBRARY OF CONGRESS CATALOGING-IN-PUBLICATION
DATA
Love Threads / Thomas Ramey Watson. p.cm.
ISBN-13: 978-0-9818430-2-5 (alk. paper)
1.Poetry, American. 2.Spirituality. 3.Symbols 4.
Signs 5.Christianity 6.Comparative Religion
I. Title.

Cover design by Cheryl Ramirez
www.CCRBookCoverDesign.com

At the round earth's imagined corners, blow
Your trumpets, angels: and arise, arise
from death, you numberless infinities
Of souls, and to your scattered bodies go . . .
                (John Donne, *Holy Sonnet 7*)

Contents

Foreword: The Point Where All Begins and Ends

Love Threads can be a painful book because it is about a hurtful relationship, but more important, it is a clear call to love and to love even when there is difficulty. A clear call to love spiritually and in body. It is essentially a transcendent calling, an ecstatic one—and a genuine journey of love.

These are poems whose obscurity win their way graciously with resonances that wistfully suggest sweetness and light without identifying many specifics or concrete manifestations of the sacred other. These poems make up invocations that appeal through the plausible and very humane nexus of dream, or vision, and longing. Continual hope for something solid that never appears or makes itself known in features that are not quite enough to satisfy a strong undercurrent of almost ambiguous desire.

The poet makes clear his romantic trajectory in the early poems. It is not long before most readers will know where they are, as long as we are amenable to some real ambiguities of image and style. The title, "Beta" of the opening poem, seems to denote, as in physics, a variable, the speaker's other coruscating from the first words of the book. Gentle images of dreaming the other reaching out in bed collide with the somewhat blunt and graphic biological terms of connection, an "umbilical" arrangement.

Making to clarify the iffy relationship, the second poem, "Aboriginal," proves the speaker believes the lover more in spirit than in person. The beloved declares a need for the freedom of love so commonly invoked, to plead connection: "Do not let me go." The triangle, if there is one emerging, is between the two in love and the spirit, which over-rides pettiness for them both. But who has not been attracted to the whims of love? Once love is tasted, that is a part of its charm. It should be solid as the experience, but it usually is not. Certainly substantiality is in pleasant question throughout.

Bring your John Donne for the third, poem, "Doing Theology," for, true to the dedication, Donne's language, "twin compasses," demands a bit of a gloss. I won't give that here, but Donne added "stiff" to the twin compasses, giving it a more edgy erotic ring. This book is only in part about erotic matters, not to take any of Donne's transcendence away from the revered subject.

And so we go as the book goes, into the thick with a kind of eroti-theological ambivalence. For I want to point out that the writer often here and in other works allows confusion of language to permeate the character and meaning of the lover, as though, sometimes, it were hard to distinguish the lover from Christ. This is a layer that I don't recognize as coming from Donne, and is solely Watson's own. Maybe this is the new metaphysical poetry of the twenty-first century. I don't know, but I read it with scrutiny and pleasure.

The fourth poem may be the best portrait of the lover, the other, "Artesian Waters." Reeds of sorrow go with waters, the stillborn child of death of hope, the confusion the speaker feels between his sorrow and the beloved's, and water, of course, made so remarkable by being dowsed for in the depths of the spirit. It's an intricate whole where some may find the reference to a "still small voice," clangs too explicitly from scripture, others right on target, but the poet is carrying the collection straight in the direction of mystical Christianity, and there is no going back. We are on track with the major resonance, and we will force our way if the images are too obscure for us now. This, of course, is both a fault in subtlety, and a strength in purpose.

"Sanctus Bells"—these words illuminate a lot about the relationship without explaining that which the speaker cannot quite explain either: "Still, that [the intertwining of past lives] does not resolve/ this peculiar vacuum/ left by knowing you're there,/ but not quite held." Central to this book of poems is the dreadful feeling of the absence of the lover, even when at hand the most intimately.

"Glossolalia" employs the phrase, "love threads/ the soul back/ into the body/ and anchors it," providing the in-text basis for the title of the book. The bodies of the lovers provide both feast and altar for the familiar communion. Less comfortable for me than the religious ecstasy is the image: "corridors dark/ and red as birth canals" early in the poem, for I know nothing of the loved other ever giving birth (as a pretext for this shocking image). In other words, the redness seems incongruous, especially in the meeting between the two in the same poem in idealized nature, among "meadows sweet/ with beebalm and honeysuckle." But all these poetic gestures are based in part on that long-lasting metaphysical music from Donne, Herbert, and the like, so a reader might expect some jarring images.

With so much intertwining of the lovers' selves and acts with God, with the solemnities and rituals of Christ, it is necessary to step back sometimes and remember that neither the speaker in the book nor his lover is really a deity. This may seem difficult sometime, with the language used, the old "religion of love," for the implications come up, as in the poem, "Driving Home": "But I repent/ to call you again." However, taken as a whole, few readers will take this as a flaw—rather, a layer, a delight.

For it is not only Christian feeling that binds the two in this book, of course—thought that permeates the most, even to rhapsodies about the nature of God and attributes of God. It is also contemporary psychology. We learn in the poem, "Shambhala," of this feature: "abuse has sharded—/ clouded/ your ability to sing." Sometimes such revelations are necessary to give earthy weight to the litanies of the divine in all this. This feature comes up several times in **Love Threads**.

Solomon had many wives, but in this book, the speaker does not garner one. Instead marriage is in the classical ideal, the marriage of minds, as in the poem, "The Wisdom of Solomon," which, while it recommends closeness, urges the lover, always hampered by past wounds, to open to God for a truer fulfillment than marriage.

The secrets of the ultimate temple of old Israel, radical, personal renewing in this world, a glass house, another garden, even a revisiting of Tao—the windup poems of this collection pull toward a general summation of spirit. The failure of the beloved to rise fully from brokenness lingers but does not seem to cause great pain. The world is as it has been in the rest of the book, but it is rather left behind—caught up in greater concerns. In some sense, these more expansive spiritual realms are also higher than the dear but desperate strife of the journey of the troubled relationship itself. They are the Alpha from which the entire journey begins. And where it ends.

Alan Naslund, author of *Silk Weather*

Beta

Never denting the bed
with the weight of that body
like airy gold
you twice clung to me
in dream time like a child.

So I smile ironically
when you say goodbye
and reach but hardly touch
and mutter that I am getting
more than most.

Dwelling in double space—
both earth and heaven—
double time—what is
and what is not—
at least not yet—
I feel a link
already deeper
than the umbilical of finger,
bone, and sinew.

Aboriginal

You say
you do not want to be alone,
then walk to the door,
not to return that night.

Except in spirit.
Again you appear,
as if drawn
by a thread of gold
and this time,
head on my chest,
voice your great need.
"Do not let me go."

Doing Theology

I too will meditate
on the meanings
radiating from our conjunction.
Whether you
will turn from orbit—
rather than
my becoming a comet—
or whether we'll enjoy
union
that permits souls
to remain fixed,
while bodies,
like twin compasses,
circle—
remains theoretical.

But I have made my promise.
In the shimmering night—
this primary state
where souls know
the alchemy of love—
I wait for you.

Artesian Waters

1

Perhaps—
but perhaps you chose this body
not so that you'd not be alone
but that all might see
that physical attraction
is not sufficient.

2

You've slept so long
that you weep when I tell you
what you've revealed
in dream,
when all the eyes of being
open like peonies,
their nectar
having drawn healing,
like the helping ant, near.

3

Your sadness reaches
like your hand—
there,
clutched in you for a moment,
I perceive that you've arched
into the doorway:
no longer alone,
your deep beauty has drawn me
through space and time
in a curved line.

4

Clenched in your belly
like a stillborn child
lies your sorrow.
At first thinking it my own,
I recognized the pain as yours:
the notes greener
and more reedy.

5

Today I heard your joy,
welling like sweet water
that you'd dowsed
but lost,
years ago.

6

Now
here, in the still, small voice,
the point
of all that is
and was and will be,
the word still bubbles still
still, Come.

Augustinian Sign Theory

Turning to find you
not in your accustomed place
in the bed beside me,
I looked to see
you throwing yourself like dice
to rend your garments
on the altar of a mind,
which, like a spider,
climbs toward the yolk
of the universe
and spins
into a black hole
where all falls in.

Come, I said,
recalling the pledge.
You came.
We slept.

I woke to write poems
and you, some hours later,
to work on book reviews,
the word still multiplying
in many mouths,
some in fuller echo,
some partial.

Come—
the sun's up,
the table's spread—
communion.

Soul Retrieval

When those men plowed you,
they helped to carve out
gardens from your soul,
like cynicism
bulldozing the rain forests
for gain.

Left intact,
the meridians that reside
like the warp and woof
of Gaea's loom
lend medicines
that heal the body
as the soul.
Disturbed,
the circulation
carries sickness,
as swift and strong as Ebola.

But restoration has begun.
Green sprouts—
quetzals and white-faced monkeys
feast on mangos and papayas—

Sanctus Bells

You had another friend
who heard you
call
across an unfamiliar city
in a land as foreign
as earth to many seems.

Why I am tuned
like a radio
to your frequency
stretches me
to perfect pitch.

Perhaps past lives
make us tuning forks
that ring sympathetically
when the other is struck.
Centuries of closeness
couldn't help but pitch us so.

Still, that does not resolve
this peculiar vacuum
left by knowing you're there,
but not quite held.

Glossolalia

1

Through corridors dark
and red as birth canals,
I call to you of vistas that open
onto meadows sweet
with bee balm and honeysuckle.
There the picnic has been laid
with wine and bread,
olives and cheese.

2

Singing, love threads
the soul
into the body
and anchors it
at the heart.
Now the chakras
can be balanced,
the wounds healed
by light that winds
like a caduceus
up the spine
and crowns you.

3

Those fingers
that could no longer play
find strength and grace
in the mind now tuned.

Here
here are the songs and symphonies
marked before birth
by your light-bearing soul
and name.

We'll play them—
our bodies the altars
from which love feeds.

Tuning

Waking several times,
I found you on me,
stretching the length of my body.
Curling my arms and legs
about you,
I would hold you there,
just as you first held
my hand —my soul—
cupped in yours
and gave me drink.

I whispered,
now remember this,
remember when you wake,
as if to weave a shining garment
to wear you to eternal day.

Now that you've
returned to your body
do you recall,
does your soul still resonate—
deep, low, in tune—
knowing it's found
a place within me
like a reed?

Yield

Sweet, languid Monday.
On Tuesday
I shared the turns,
the fleeting doubts,
the mind's falls—
even love's surges.

The joy returns,
its tendrils
sprouting like hair.

Every night,
our senses restored
by that subtle knot
my chest feels more and more
your pillow.

Intuitive faculty—
higher than discursive reason—
is angels' food,
the dazzling darkness
that mystics say is God's.

Stretching into days now,
I hardly know
whose song we sing,
whose fingers play.

Learning to Prophesy

When Pluto stole her,
Persephone was bending
in a field
to recite the names
of flowers—
some with looks familiar,
some barely recognizable.

That we might learn
a rather unknown tongue,
we stood
parsing sentences,
struggling
with vocabulary.

Feeling more advanced,
I began to babble
about meanings
which had sprouted.

But without proficiency,
all tongues—
whether Russian, French, Swahili—
remain sounds—
faces
glimpsed through glass,
some dark
across a plain.

Harrowing

Like Orpheus,
I would descend
to where you weep,
fled
from all who would pursue
and pluck you
the finest flower
of earth's meadows.
In song's brilliance
you'd bud again.

Like Christ,
I'd search
the darkest realms
for just your soul.
Finding its light
alloyed by baser metals,
flickering and cobalt,
we'd tune our wings,
making every turn and lifting his.

Now
I come to fields
with bachelor's buttons
woven
among the golds and greens
and hesitate,
hoping for a glimpse of you—
your voice,
        your eyes

so deep,
        so blue.

Hermeneutics

You thrust your gospel
into my breast.
I took it up and read.
The story ipecac,
with hints of honey
that barely brushed
the tongue.
Darkness,
tomb clothes
always before dawn.
Familiar
with the course of plotting,
I held no expectant breath.

But this.
Oh physician—
turn—
and in healing me,
I heal you.

Driving Home

Pulse racing,
I focus on the trumpet—
slow, low, bluesy.
Wipers slap
as tires hydroplane.

Rhythms out of synch,
I'll give you up:
it's never good to bind
one who cannot give.

The trumpeter inserts
the copper cup mute.
Sound darker,
insistent—
opening—
driving upwards—
scaling notes and octaves—
oh heavens
glory.

Illuminating,
like lightning in the east:
Not mistaken
I know the fire
in me
is your fire too.

In the Sistine,
God reaches
toward Adam's hand.

We looked up:
your face
lights the entire chapel.

Smooth Sailing

When, after weeks,
I hear from you,
you whisper your distress,
how your bronchia tightened,
how you're afraid to breathe
and start the blood again.

I recall
how I broke my pledge,
making it hard for you to come.
When you broke through,
twice you told me so yourself.
I was busy with my book, I said—
then confessed that
I gave you distance
because you never called,
because my messages
seemed dropped into bottles
bobbing toward shores
ever more distant,
ever more faint.
No sirens' song,
no dark arts for me.

But I repent
to call you again,
weaving soul's health,
while you return to my bed,
ever more amorous,
your lungs filling once more
with breath,

my lungs
filling like sails
once more with you.

Solstice

Though summer
with its searing sun
has returned
and even
white rose buds
look as if a blow torch
were turned on them,
sparrows and robins sing
as if no summer but this
existed,
ever enjoyed.

My own heart recalls
tunes and words
I'd thought forgotten
many turns before—
even sweeter
than when we watched
the kingfisher light
to calm both land and sea.
Halcyon days—
brought by souls' delight
and night's sweet mystery.

The Curvature of Space and Time

When you leave the body,
you rise,
turning
to the right—
or to the left.
And then you're out.

My arms around you
your soul turned into me,
showing
how angels merge,
spirits blending,
a higher form of sex:
what humans
intuit,
long for—
you a dolphin
inside a sea—

how we,
with our turns and falls,
prove nothing
can move long
in a straight line,
all sounding
God's geometry.

Sacred Geometry

Look again
at the circle,
no irregularity,
no beginning,
no end.
Alchemical symbol for gold,
reflection and expansion
of the point
that God is —
the center
of all motion,
whether straight, circular,
or spiral.

You find such rings
around God's arms,
around his neck—
bracelets of the warrior,
adornments of the gods—
also around Saturn,
ruler of a golden age,
and ringed planet—
and, as you point out,
around the third fingers
of our souls' left
and star-strewn hands.

No Longer Alone Indeed

Just before dawn
I felt your soul depart
from its place with mine.
Falling asleep again,
I woke to find
the bed shaking
from what I surmised the dog
kicking against the mattress.

The thumping that I felt
now in my groin—
your groin, that is—
revealed your pleasure
there, as I related
on Thursday morning
shortly after seven.

When, some minutes later,
I felt the body descend
into the warm bath
I knew we had achieved more
from our strengthening of souls:
our bodies too were shared.

Shambhala

She takes my hand,
reads my fretting—
finds you in the pulse—
remarks on wisdom gained
through many lives.
A teacher now,
perfectionist, cool,
of great beauty.
Wherever you turn,
you bless
 and dispense charm,
even rice and saffron.

She remarks how
when she saw you
as Buddha
in persimmon, pomegranate,
kiwi, grape, and melon
silks and satins,
teaching in temples—
me at your side,
she couldn't read—
male—female—male—turns again—
the dancer—dance—
echoes down corridors of mirrors.
But abuse has sharded
your ability to sing.

Under the Throne
(Rev. 9)

At last you've confessed the root
of your lower chakra wounding,
which I called to attention
but didn't know the cause.

More than the teasing peacock
who was my uncle,
your man soon knew
every minutiae
of your fledging body,
barnyard where he rooted.

In the shrouded box
where you slipped each day
to chirp gladly to the Father,
you were pointed
to the Archetype,
watching landlord,
who would make you pay
every penny
that by omission
or commission
you owed.

Learning
that if you kept fathers busy
with grains
strewn in the way before them
they would not notice broken wings,
you easily confessed

fear and loneliness
before you'd trust me
as priest
of your twisted heart.

Lights and Candles

Before the calendar was changed,
this, the longest night of every year,
was watched by St. Lucy,
who chose to have her eyes gouged out
before she'd lose insight.

To recall this day's saint,
that I, so aptly named,
might leave behind
seared branches, brittle leaves,
and rest again,
I draw blinds,
check the clock,
and light a fire,
four candles and an oil lamp
wreathed with pine and fir branches,
to commemorate all illumination—
reflections of primary light.

When angels
from the east and west
and north and south
take up their trumpets
and wing on wing
and wheel in wheel
ascends,
I'll hold you once again—
embodiment of all—
healing all wounds
and fleshing soul
with eyes.

So Much Concern with Hair

Whether in the wrong place,
or wrong color,
some would sing the body
in commemoration
of beauty, wisdom,
or life's varied course—
but you worry,
shave and die them black—
too young—untenured—
to reveal not just graying temples
but shocks of white,
with me again confessor.

But if indeed your priest,
I must admonish kindly:
pluck darkness from within,
dear one,
so that our souls be white.

Testing

Obliquely answering,
you end your letter
saying that you believe
your soul a little devil
playing tricks.
Probably, you say,
you feel so much stabler
and happier than in years
because I've forced you
to face issues head on
with help of friends.

Puzzled by my "confusion"
of the spiritual and the physical,
which, for you, are separate realms,
you argue for continued distance
between bodies,
our souls linked.
This serendipitous arrangement—
Fate, you say—
will no doubt spin
for a long while,
regardless of our wills.

Like that little devil
you think your soul,
I must banish you
to darkness
where you will know the pain
of being forsaken, alone, again.

Cast out, realize
how seven
more horrid than the first
come in.

But with this redeeming wisdom:
our time united can provide
the touchstone
by which gold is known.

Emblems

When my friends performed Reiki,
they remarked on the frozen zone
between my shoulder blades.
The energy felt humplike.

The sudden lipoma
that appeared on my dog's chest
just after you and I met
rose to mind—
how quickly it grew from sternum
to right armpit, impeding his step.
Perhaps his
was my hump, after all.

But no, one friend said,
it felt as though something—
some kind of being—
had taken residence there,
just behind my heart and lungs,
hiding like a fetus
who wished to be unborn.

Suddenly, I called you—
infuse my body,
join soul and soul
so toe and finger
bone and vessel
feels yours and mine,
full grown.

Planted by the Moon

Like a milkweed seed
unable to root
in the din
of your body,
your soul took flight
wishing to locate
a fecund medium.

Angry not at me
but at my friends
who made me know
that I could not allow
you to unfurl tendrils
like explorer's flags in me,
you appear to my waking self
to cultivate sympathy.

Opening my almanac,
I read that all has phases:
you must come next
when your body shines
with light that is your own.
Then we'll plant
a garden that's neither
mine nor yours.

In the Dark

Because I've known where you stood
or sat when your soul went back—
how you felt—
even what you've said—
I began to grow suspicious
that my muffled ears and laryngitis
that for months have visited
like unwelcome relatives
who leave but then return
were perhaps shared too,
part of our common life.

Opening Mark's gospel,
I found Jesus casting darkness
from a boy
brought by his father,
who spoke and heard
the words of life.

Jesus answered failed disciples
that such spirits
are removed
by faith and prayer.

While I will bind darkness
on your behalf,
that your soul
might infuse your body—
with resurrection
that befits your name—

I'll also whisper
to your soul
no longer housed
with mine:
stand up and free yourself
from this strong man
who's taken you captive—
from this world's spirit
of the deaf and dumb.

Conundrums

As if in mirror
on mirror
on mirror,
questions
that echo
through centuries
to all
still haunt us.

But why
would the soul
who's learned
the truths of Lent
choose carnival again?

To show that physical beauty
is not sufficient
seems hardly worth perils
that disembody the soul—
even for redeeming
linked souls—
especially those
of parents, friends, lovers
who've loved long
not reality,
but images
of desire.
And only that.

Were our motions
circumscribed—
by God
      or us
           or both—
long before I saw
and heard you call,
girding myself to lay
those real wounds open
before applying
love's atoning salve?

Purgatorial States

Concentrate
on this point,
this life—here, now—
expand—
like God—
to fill all vacuums.

If possible,
I would prefer one life—
not this, necessarily.
But since embodied
in late twentieth century,
an American enduring
the test of empire,
I must accept this drama—
so that either here,
or in some further realm,
I do not try
screw and rack,
and vomit food
that's tainted.

Walk-ins

Instead of the usual
assassination of flesh,
some souls,
weary of life assignments,
give title to their bodies
to others
seeking entrance.
So much tidier than
waiting in darkness,
crying and puking,
crawling and tipping
each step Herculean.

This time,
some disembodied vow,
there'll be no forgetting
the clouds of glory
that they once knew.

Others who hunger
for touch and smell and genitals
will jump the gates,
already gnawing,
to devour
all experience,
every body that yields
to Siren's songs—
till spinning,
all becomes performance.

Anima

Once more, Baltho sleeps
nearest the wall—your side—
where you felt safe—
then moves to rest
on my feet.
.

While your soul remained,
this dog stayed on the floor,
sensing a presence
that made the bed
too small for three.

No longer welcome
to come and stay,
you know
the door's ajar.

When Balthazar
kicks and groans,
I quicken—
hoping that soul
has taken residence
in body.
Then I'll hold you
whole.

The Wisdom of Solomon

Arcane lore says
history's great
hold two souls within.
In harmony,
such souls ennoble,
lending the strength
and insight
that all good marriages hold.
In discord, the tortured—
Hitlers, Attilas, and Amins—
are fashioned.
Yet, all inhabit clay.

Having gained entrance
through your lower chakras,
fear, shame,
confusion,
like the counterfeiting potter,
would wrest your body
into an idol,
choking you
with poisoned air.

While I would welcome
your soul with me,
together drawing music
of the spheres within,
I'd ring false
if I did not argue
you return

and turn yourself
to the source of breath eternal.
Although he lets us
sound in shameful temples,
what he inspires
can ring again.

Urim and Thummim

If one dares entrance
into the inner sanctum
one must dress in garments
of one kind,
without double
or blended mind,
clean, tied
with purple sash
wearing breastplate
jeweled with virtues won
on earth and heavens—
past porch—through
sixty-six cubits
of the holy place,
then venturing thirty-three—
thrice-washed
both in and out.

The scarlet thread
tells true.
If clean, the wool is bleached
white as the hairs
of those whose wisdom
has approached God's.
If not, the priest is struck
as if by lightning.
All in twos and threes.

2

Neither Solomon's
nor Harod's Temples
now stand,
their destruction
a half-millennium apart.

Solely fulfilled,
the one high priest fit
to enter and remain:
having died —
his raiment—
virtues—
tested,
always single-minded,
white.

Like souls,
the spirit
of this high priest
enjoys
many habitations.
The search for temples
built of stone
or flesh,
is vain.

So come,
let him breathe
in you and me.

In him
there is no

ignis fatuus,
only *lux eternam.*

Scape

A footpath —
beside a winding gorge,
a river rushes below
its waters strong
to pierce the hardest ground.
An ancient, garden city,
of varied stones and tiles,
snakes the other side.

I walk alone,
sighting mountains
lit by sunlight—
distant—
behind the stony walls.

The drop steep—
near—the path
brings no caught breath:
having learned,
if desired, to walk
as though I touch the ground,
I wind, confident
that I will reach
the other side.

A natural joining—
but without footpath,
just rope.
In my hands,
it seems

but string—
though strong.

I swing
to another rope—
no thicker—
grasp,
as if an athlete,
feeling muscles strain,
pull up
to the city side.

The way—
the bookstore,
large, but cozy—
the crowd—
mostly women,
some men.

Arriving shortly,
you stand,
smiling, at my side.
I sign.

Glass Houses

From a mica-like translucence
the panes clear
to a milk-glass clarity,
where the blurred shapes
that move as in a dream
and cast shadows
that are rarely direct
finally fill in.

Now, we can read the lines
that mark both palms
and faces.
See—this is where
despair wrote
in dark calligraphy upon her.
This is where his joy
spanned
from palm to palm.

This is the house
where all must come to dwell.
Like skin, these panes stretch
and miraculously fill in.

A New Earth

1

After restoration of your soul,
the dangers of the trek
became apparent—
even to your soul—
which buzzed nearby
last night.

We knew
that continents
which had split and slid
across vast seas
had to reunite
if wholeness be achieved.
How languages would change,
which vocabulary would remain—
still territory unexplored—
because omniscient
nor omnipresent
is either of our souls.

2

Knowing my need,
and reminding me
that everything must turn,
you spoke of growing consciousness,
how the once-light soul
feels—
        to both of us—
heavier, solider—honeyed:
it fully habits flesh.

Better knowing
my dearth
and your ability
to garden,
you assure me,
melts the general frost,
bringing consciousness
to flower—
a new and hybrid genus,
pollinated by both.

Cosmos

Days. Nights. Seasons.
All have their turnings.
Like wheel in wheel.

Where we know as we are known
we see as we are seen.
All things are known. All seen.

This is the gathering. The harvest.
The place where shrieking stops
and angels feed.

Tao

After long journeying
we arrive at the core,
the source we've dreamed—
where all that's sought
has found its level,
flows, supports,
smoothing the sharp stone's edge.

Our bodies like buoys,
voice announces completion
of all we've wished, and dared.

My breath, I say—
is my breath, you say—
Deeper. Extending.
Your breath,
my breath. Omega.
Worlds spinning.

All Comes to This

This is the house at land's end,
where the waters of a thousand oceans
lap the shores of a thousand thousand lands:
familiar, a hologram
dreamed a thousand times
by a thousand voices.

This dwelling, this house,
yes it is the place where we have—
where we will dwell.
The great windows, like eyes,
overlook the sea,
watching the ebb and flow.

Suddenly,
we stand inside, hands linked
in a mandala
of warmth, light.
We sit on a couch
that is long and wide,
without horizon.
We lie on a bed of varicolored feathers.
Alpha. Alpha. Our hearts say—
Alpha.

Acknowledgements

The following poems in this collection were first published as follows:
"All Comes to This," in *Earthlight,* 2000.
"Artesian Waters," in *Christian Century*, 1997.

I wish to thank a number of people who have helped me with my poetry in particular. Sena Jeter Naslund and Alan Naslund have both proved insightful editors and colleagues, whom I have known since graduate school. They have helped place my work in several venues. Fellow poet and editor Jill Baumgaertner has long been supportive of my work, seeing that it got published in several magazines and journals. I also owe a debt of gratitude to poets Maxine Kumin and Stephen Spender, with whom I worked for a time in graduate school.

These poems record a series of experiences mostly in the realm of the soul that I had for over a year in the late 1990s. In its way it reflects and serves as a tribute to Donne, Herbert, Vaughan, Milton, Blake, Wordsworth, and various mystics, including those of other traditions, who have been my mentors.

About the Author

One of Thomas Ramey Watson's prominent forebears on his mother's side was Jacques LaRamee. A number of places in the upper Rocky Mountain West bear his name to this day. Laramie, Wyoming is best known. Jacques was a renowned and influential explorer and fur trapper. Because he was just, honest, and treated others, including the often-despised native Americans, well, he was held in high esteem. One winter, the story goes, the native Americans were starving, so they killed one of Ramee's cattle. He told his workers not to say anything—they were hungry. Jacques shared with fellow free trappers his theory that the world was wide and there was room enough for all. He had the courage to live his convictions and followed the beat of his own heart, not what was imposed on him from outside.

One of Ramee's progeny, psychotherapist, life coach, writer, and professor, Thomas Ramey Watson believes that journeying in various realms—of the mind, the physical world, and the soul—is central to enjoying a good life. The insights gleaned from becoming aware of the intersecting planes of existence lead us to fuller and more deeply lived lives.

Thomas Ramey Watson, Ph.D., is an affiliate faculty member of Regis University's College of Professional Studies in Denver, Colorado. He has served as the Episcopal chaplain (lay) for the Auraria Campus in Denver and taught English for the University of Colorado at Denver. He has trained as a psychotherapist and was named a Research Fellow at Berkeley Divinity School at Yale University, a position he did not take, choosing to do postdoctoral work at Cambridge University instead.

He is the author of many scholarly writings, including an acclaimed book on Milton, *Perversions, Originals, and Redemptions in* Paradise Lost.

Dr. Watson is available for speaking engagements, teaching assignments, counseling, and coaching. His web address is
www.thomasrameywatson.com,
and he can be reached at
trw@thomasrameywatson.com.

You are welcome to join his Facebook pages:
www.facebook.com/thomas.watson.790
www.facebook.com/BalthoTheDogWhoOwnedAMan

The first chapter of Thomas Ramey Watson's popular memoir *Baltho, The Dog Who Owned a Man*:

Embracing Mystery

One giant leap—and his front paws landed on my chest. As he stared into my eyes, and I gazed into his, I knew this was the Afghan hound who had been calling me telepathically for weeks. This time, I felt him physically.

I was standing just outside the Denver Afghan Rescue. "You're here," I whispered, sensing his presence. I surveyed the grounds. Dry, tiny-leaved, Chinese elms dabbed a landscape of sagebrush and sand beneath the blazing June sun. "I know it." I walked toward the twelve-foot high, chain-link fence that surrounded the compound, giving it the air of a correctional facility.

As I neared the fence, pebbles crunched underfoot. I opened the gate and walked toward a small, wood-frame house on the west side of the grounds. Dozens of dogs barked, alerting each other and their caretakers to an intruder. I could make out the individual voices of at least fifteen dogs housed there—medium-to-low-range sounds of alarm. Their collective din was excruciating.

A man looked out the window of the house. The door opened. He stepped out into the sunlight and strode my way. He stood at least six-feet-three. He sized me up from head to foot and smiled. I guessed he was Jim, the head of the Rescue—the man I'd talked with last night on the phone. "I'm Jim." He extended his hand. His grip was firm. "Mystery's a super-sized Afghan, weighing seventy-five pounds," he said. "With the build of a linebacker, you ought to be able to handle him. You're what, six-two, maybe two-twenty?"

"Not quite—one ninety-eight."

"Well, you're big enough not to get knocked down." He looked me over again. "Maybe suffer a shoulder dislocation, but only now and then."

I laughed, hoping he was making a joke.

The name the Rescue had given the Afghan hound, Mystery, felt significant. My life was one of paradoxes and mysteries too. If we come into this life with a map, mine was one of roundabouts and detours, with few straight roads anywhere. I was at the Afghan Rescue because I hadn't been able to elude the notion that an Afghan hound was telepathically calling me, begging me, to locate and rescue him. An independent, high-maintenance Afghan wasn't the dog that I'd been planning to adopt. I'd wanted one of those popular breeds—a bouncy, responsive Golden Retriever or a Labrador.

"Mystery's down at the other end," Jim said, walking me out to the pens on the east side of the property. "You said on the phone you're a psychotherapist?" He lifted the heavy padlock on the gate, stuck in a key, and released the lock. He swung open the gate.

I nodded. "I'm just about finished with my training. Until recently, I taught English and was the Episcopal chaplain for the Auraria campus." It was 1992. The glare of the sun on the cement runs and concrete doghouses inside the individual cages made me wish I'd worn sunglasses.

"Good," Jim began. "You're complicated. You should be able to understand Mystery, if anyone can." He laughed.

"I've spent my whole life trying to understand mysteries," I said. "It seems something is always trying to outfox us, threatening our best-laid plans. I'd like to see what's ahead and avert the danger before it manifests."

Jim laughed. He closed the gate behind us. "This reminds me—you've got to be careful about latches of every kind. Mystery is smart, often too smart. He can open just about any gate. A strong padlock—kept locked—is the only guarantee of confining him."

We passed into an alley that must have stretched at least a hundred yards ahead. Individual kennels formed by six-foot high chain-link fencing lined the way. Each kennel was maybe eight-feet wide and twelve-feet deep and contained a square dog house made of cement at the back. Some kennels held one or two Afghans. Some were empty.

As we walked, I spotted a frail, small-boned, white Afghan. *There's a Snow Queen in hiding*, I thought. Her body was shaking. She stared up at me with brown, soulful eyes. She looked pitiful, so needy. The rescuer in me wanted to respond.

"The dog for you is this way," Jim said, urging me on. He was several yards ahead of me by then. The place was a labyrinth. I wondered where the Minotaur was.

We took a few more steps, and a huge, dark beast bounded from a distant side-run into our path. His long, brindle hair, as I'd learned to call it during my earlier years with an Afghan, flew from his sides like magnificent wings.

"Mystery's out!" Jim shouted—as the Afghan bounded past him toward me, barking excitedly.

I had only time to mutter, "Mystery's everywhere," before he skidded, reared up, and, with his front paws, landed on my chest. Remarkably, he was so graceful that he didn't knock me over. I did, however, feel the impact of his muscle-driven mass.

Still barking—then whimpering and yapping alternately, as if he'd found his long-lost partner and friend—he nipped at my nose, my earlobes, my chin.

"Hey," I said, "I know you're ecstatic, but take it easy with the biting. It hurts."

In the bright sunshine, his thick, dark coat showed a glossy mix of walnut browns and mahoganies, highlighted by Brazilian teaks and blonds. The hair revealed a distinct red cast.

A big white star with a long tail ran the length of his chest. His dark whiskers, also showing red highlights, formed a full and bushy beard, the greatest I'd ever sighted on an Afghan. His eyebrows must have been an inch long, and his intelligent eyes, like rich cherry wood, complemented his coat.

He began to pet me with first one paw and then the other. His toes moved upon me, massaging my skin. I noticed the huge, webbed feet that his breed had evolved. Their toes became webbed so they could gain better traction in desert sands, helping them grasp unstable terrain. Their upward-curved tails could be tracked above desert scrub.

"I think you've got yourself a dog." Jim laughed. "As soon as you leave here, you'd better search for the largest carrier crate you can find. Put Mystery in it when you aren't around. Even though we think he's five or six, he needs security. That'll keep your house safe when you're gone."

I recalled Jim's telling me on the phone that the woman who'd first adopted him said he'd ripped up her bedding and chewed a hole the size of a watermelon in the middle of her mattress. "He peed and pooped everywhere," Jim had said. "So she returned him to us."

"On the phone, you told me you knew something about Afghans, didn't you?" Jim asked. We'd already been through this, but Jim wanted assurance.

I nodded.

"They're sight hounds," he said, repeating what he'd told me earlier. "They see something and take off."

"I got my previous Afghan as soon as my divorce went through," I said. "I've long been drawn to Afghans. I don't know why. I had my Afghan, Oriana, for years."

Mystery wrapped his legs tightly around my chest, as if to hug me tight, never to let go. He fussed, whimpered happily, and yapped away. The distraction was welcome. I didn't want to dwell on the past, certainly not my bad marriage and divorce.

I looked into Mystery's eyes. "Oh dog, I know you're the one." Tears welled in my eyes. For weeks, he'd been tweaking the telepathic connection, finding my frequency.

"I need you—rescue me!" he'd broadcast. "You are mine. I am yours."

I lowered my head, so his cheek pressed against mine. "I am yours, and you are mine—for as long as we're given." By then, I could hardly speak. I hugged him tightly, gathered my wits, and opened my mouth, but the words remained only in thought. *Hello, willful, curious—beautiful—swift-as-the-wind, Afghan. Hello, Mystery, my friend.*

A preview of Thomas Ramey Watson's forthcoming novel:

Reading the Signs: A Paranormal Love Story

Synopsis

Ted Jones, university campus chaplain and English Professor in Denver, doesn't need more problems. His life has been full of them. Yet, at the beseeching of the spirit of an old woman, he becomes involved with Sharon, the woman's grown granddaughter. Damaged though she is, Sharon responds. Although Sharon and Ted's trials are multiple, their love forms the crux of the novel. Such love reaches beyond time and space as we normally conceive them, to involve intersecting planes of existence that touch both past and future.

Chapter 1: Vision

The bells of St. Elizabeth's, loud and dissonant, blended for a moment before becoming strident again. They brought back memories of studies in Italy. There, such bells rang out from the landscape and tumbled across the hills into cerulean seas. Here in Denver, the sounds reverberated across campus to snow-covered peaks and reminded me of melodies rising from chaos.

I walked toward the church. The sun shone brightly. A blizzard had blanketed the city the week before, but this morning felt warm. The snow had almost vanished, even in shaded areas. Overnight, the grass had turned from straw to dewy green. Crocuses were bursting into small purple, white, and yellow stars. Like Persephone, spring had returned from Hades, decked in flowery gowns of green. The cycle of life had begun again.

From the sidewalk in front of St. Elizabeth's, I heard a voice. It was coming from the roof. My eyes traveled up the gray granite blocks to a white statue of Mary, a bouquet of roses carved in her hand. I moved my eyes to the stained-glass window behind the statue. The voice came from there.

I stood still and concentrated. I shifted my consciousness slightly to the side. Mystical experiences were not new to me. I'd experienced a number of these phenomena over my thirty-three years. As a professor of English, I specialized in the Great Philosophical and Theological Tradition of the Western World. I'd read the mystics and saints. I was also the Episcopal chaplain for the colleges sharing the Auraria campus.

The apparition of an old woman floating in mid-air appeared near the rose window, a smaller version of those adorning the great cathedrals of Europe. Like a mist moving across the building, her body looked translucent, as fragile as rice paper. Her white hair was pinned at the back, with loose strands falling about the deep wrinkles of her face. Again, she called my name and began to speak in a

language that sounded like Russian. She gestured for me to
come closer.

From Thomas Ramey Watson's book of poetry, *The Necessity of Symbols*:

Foreword: What Body?

You still believe the body is a temple for the spirit? Then read Thomas Ramey Watson and be delighted and appalled with him! *The Necessity of Symbols* plays again and again on the sacredness of the body—the body in love, the body in ecstasy of spirit and memory, even the body of Christ in communion.

Like the forgotten troubadours, the poet gives a credible poetic ground that loving the beloved's body is close to loving God, or at least appreciating the universe. "Knot Intrinsicate" celebrates a woman's power:

I am seventeen—
you, soft-voiced Guenevere.
But a Russian doll,
you held inside Mary,
hawk of Catholicism,
and Cleopatra,
salad of the crescent world:
eaten—undone—whole again.

In a long poem that summarizes loss of job, loss of wife, loss of environment (Colorado), the poet holds psalms and songs in memory step by step of the way, shoring up the many threats to his spiritual life ("A Book of Hours"):

My mind
stayed on echoes:
whether one eats

God's words,
or wakes
within them—
does upheaval
always follow?

In the poem, "Holy Communion," the poet does not scruple to equate the host with two lovers, who, as the poem progresses are separated, however, with the finite limits between them implicitly contrasted to God's infinite love: "Broken from you, / I am set on a shelf." However, the lover remains an inspiration:

Rising
past the fragrance of ankles and thighs,
lingering on chest and neck, to pause
on tiny moles like cinnamon
sprinkled about your mouth

that explored with words, and tongue,
and smile, then to those eyes,
brown as buttered crust on fresh-baked bread;
still I hear your voice, yeasty, low.

These are fine points of a book with a broad sweep—poems about family, poems contrasting the poet's native Denver with the signal cultural meccas of Europe, poems most often of joy. The range is admirable and the poems intricate and dedicated to spiritual growth, with creation the touchstone where reality is tested and embodied.

Alan Naslund, author of *Silk Weather*

www.ingramcontent.com/pod-product-compliance
Lightning Source LLC
Chambersburg PA
CBHW020950030426
42339CB00004B/38